BABY DOLLS
AND THEIR CLOTHES

To Silvia and Eros with love and gratitude

ACKNOWLEDGEMENTS

Special thanks to Ersilia for the stencil decoration on the cradle on pages 128-129.
Thanks to Daelli Arte e Gioco – Via Porro Lambertenghi 34, Milan, which kindly supplied us with the stockinet necessary for making the dolls in this book.
To Fiorucci Department Store – Galleria Passerella 1, Milan which kindly lent us the cloth animals.

Editor Cristina Sperandeo
Photography Alberto Bertoldi and Mario Matteucci
Graphic design and layout Paola Masera and Amelia Verga
Translation Chiara Tarsia

© 1996 RCS Libri S.p.A, Milan

Martingale & Company
PO Box 118
Bothell, WA 98041-0118 USA
www.martingale-pub.com

Printed in Italy
05 04 03 02 01 00   6 5 4 3 2 1

Library of Congress Cataloging-in-Publication Data Is Available.

Mission Statement
We are dedicated to providing quality products and service by working together to inspire creativity and to enrich the lives we touch.

BABY DOLLS
AND THEIR CLOTHES

Dozens of Projects to Make

Valeria Ferrari

BOTHELL, WASHINGTON

TABLE OF CONTENTS

INTRODUCTION

First the little legs, then the arms with the hands only faintly hinted at, followed by a tiny body, a little ungainly, perhaps, but ever so soft, and lastly a small, round face with two smiling blue eyes and long, chestnut hair. While from my grandmother's deft hands there appeared, as if by magic, a rag doll, we children would think up different ways of making clothes out of old garment remnants for our new playmate.

Many years have passed since the days when the charm of childhood and the tenderness of love were represented for my sisters and me by those sweet little creatures which granny used to make. They were unique dolls, made just for us, shaped according to our fantasy and imagination, at whose birth we would assist with the excitement and awe which turn those moments into unforgettable memories.

And then things changed.

Plastic got the upper hand, fads influenced children's tastes, and only that which was advertised on television or showcased in toyshop windows began to appear beautiful and desirable.

Today, making things with one's hands seems to be back in fashion: there is an ever-increasing number of people who love making objects which are personalized, unique, and steeped in affection for the intended recipient. And what other objects lend themselves better to communicating love and affection than rag dolls?

This is the reason it was natural for me to think back to my granny's dear old hands, to remember her movements, the practical tricks of the trade which come with experience, to hear her encouragement once more.

However, I did not want this great legacy to remain confined solely to my family. I wanted to make it available to all those people who, like me, have a passion for the dear old things of the past—lovers of needlecraft and period dolls, mothers who want their children's toys to be made of soft, natural materials, fathers eager to liven up parties with puppets depicting the characters of the world's favorite fairy tales. This book is dedicated to all these people. Now a grandmother, I wrote this book with the help of my students, who were only too happy to impart their knowledge and joy to other mothers and children.

Dollmaking does not require any particular skill, although those of you who can sew are naturally at an advantage. The mothers who take my classes generally obtain good results at first go.

The patterns offered in this book range from "primitive" dolls, made from skeins of wool, to more elaborate ones with finely-shaped heads. It is up to you to choose which to make, according to the needs of your child.

What is important for a small child, for example, is not so much the realism of the doll as the feeling of tenderness it provokes: a child would probably prefer a doll with a vaguely defined body, soft to touch and to hug in bed while dozing off to sleep, rather than an extremely beautiful doll.

With the passing of time, the child's observation skills will sharpen until it will be more satisfying to play with a doll with a well-defined face, whose clothes can be changed. You can accompany your child's growth, making all those things that will gradually be needed.

Remember, however, that the aim of rag dolls is not that of "copying" reality, but rather of exciting feelings of tenderness, of developing one's imagination.

A vaguely defined face will give the child the possibility of deciding each time whether the doll is crying, laughing, or sleeping: in other words, the possibility of feeling in tune with the doll.

To talk of the philosophic importance of toys would be inappropriate. Just turn your mind back to your own childhood: your favorite doll was probably not the most attractive one, the one able to cry or talk, but the one perhaps a little old and dirty, but ever so soft, which you would hug before falling asleep. The doll your child will cherish the most will probably be the one she has seen you making: tender, sweet and made with love. It will be unique in the world, just like your child.

HOW TO USE THIS BOOK

This book offers a varied array of rag dolls: dolls made from skeins of wool, knitted dolls, dolls made with flesh-colored fabric and a well-defined head.

You will find that these dolls all require about the same skill level to make. The time required for each one, however, differs considerably: it could take you from 30 minutes to make a doll from skeins of wool, to 20 hours for one made of fabric with embroidered eyes and hair.

The estimated time required is mentioned at the beginning of each project, although your actual time may depend on the materials used, as well how quickly you like to work. Each pattern can be made smaller, taller, fatter, slimmer or softer— whichever strikes your

fancy. The patterns supplied must be enlarged: you can photocopy them, enlarging them to the size you prefer. Bear in mind, however, that a doll is usually approximately 11 3/4" to 13 3/4" tall. With just a few touches to the pattern or to the padding, your dolls can take on quite a different look. For example, a newborn will have a large head and a chubby body; a small child a round face, while that of a slightly "older" child will be longer. The hairstyle is also important: use long braids for more adult dolls and a bob cut or pony tails for the younger ones. With regards to the doll's wardrobe, this book offers a wide range of easy-to-make patterns. Be careful in choosing colors and materials: a doll dressed in soft, pastel-hued garments creates a different effect to one dressed in strong colors and stiff fabrics. You will also find instructions on how to make rag toys.

MATERIALS

To make the dolls, you'll need to have the following supplies on hand.

Patterns: Lightweight card stock, tissue paper, and pencil.

Fabrics: Cotton and felt fabric scraps for clothing, plus cotton doubleknit fabric for the sculpted doll heads and bodies. You'll need about 1/2 yard per doll. (If you have difficulty finding doubleknit [sometimes called stockinet], you can use a tee shirt. But if your aim is to make a robust doll, it's best to search for cotton doubleknit at a fabric shop.)

Notions: Ribbons, laces, woolen yarn for hair, sewing needles, an 8"-10" doll needle, strong thread for hand sewing, such as quilting or carpet thread, and scissors. You'll also need buttons for trimming clothing and narrow elastic for waistlines.

Stuffing: White or off-white woolen yarn, and wool quilt batting or polyfil.

Finishing: Chalks or wax pastels for giving color to the cheeks and color pencils for drawing the eyes and mouth complete your tool kit.

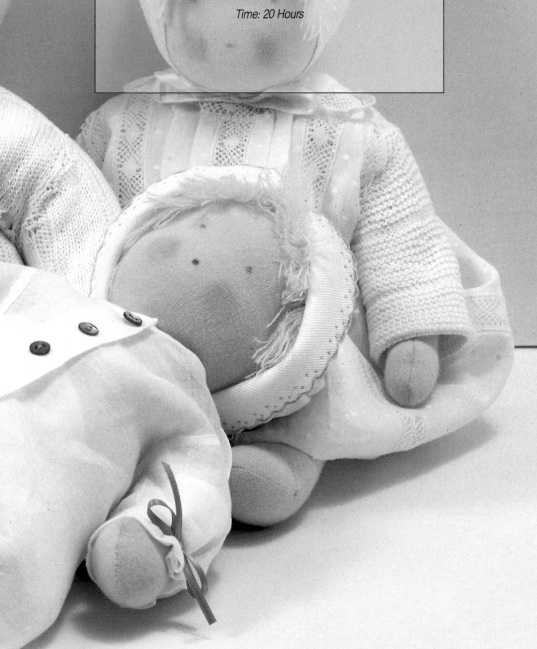

MAKING A DOLL

Time: 20 Hours

THE INSIDE OF THE HEAD

1

You will need:
- Doubleknit fabric or sock or elastic gauze for bandages
- Wool yarn and wool quilt batting
- Needle and strong thread

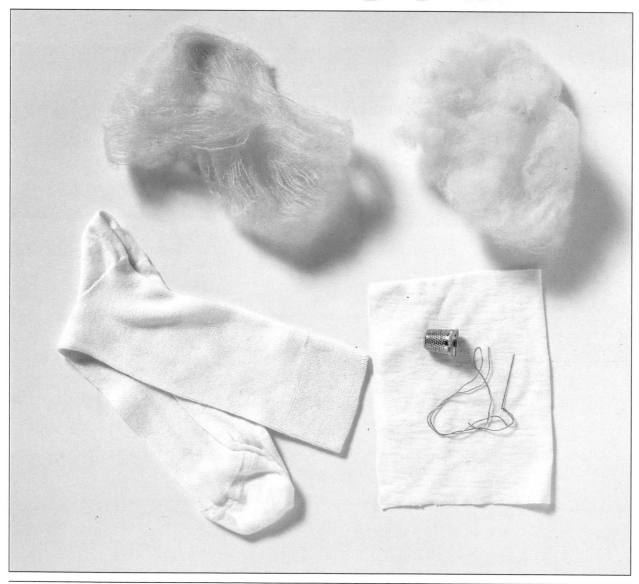

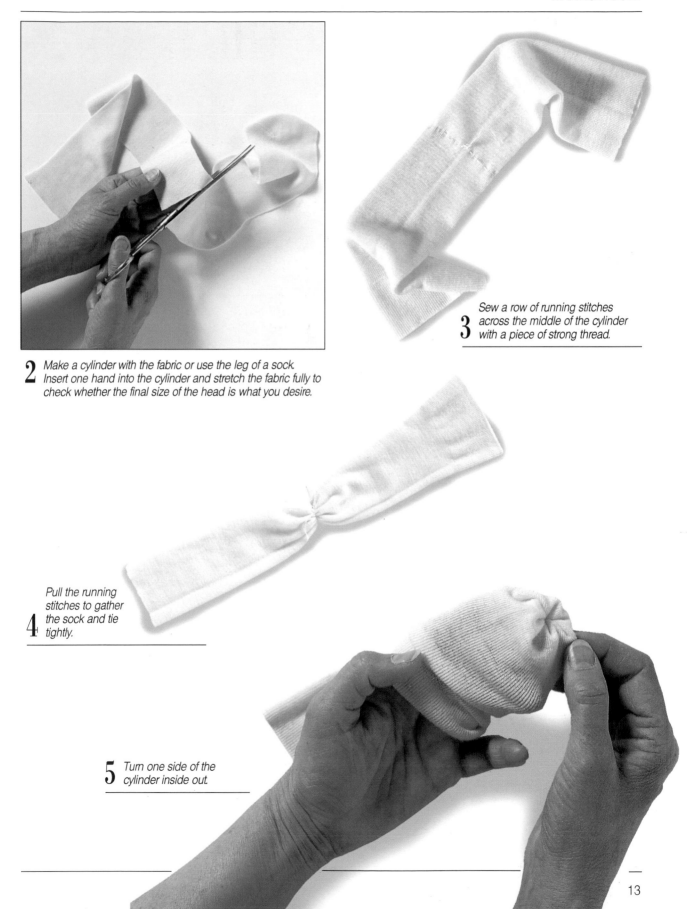

2 Make a cylinder with the fabric or use the leg of a sock. Insert one hand into the cylinder and stretch the fabric fully to check whether the final size of the head is what you desire.

3 Sew a row of running stitches across the middle of the cylinder with a piece of strong thread.

4 Pull the running stitches to gather the sock and tie tightly.

5 Turn one side of the cylinder inside out.

6 You should now have an even, closed rosette on the top of the cylinder.

7 Make a tight ball of white wool yarn. This will serve as the core of the head and will give stability to the shape.

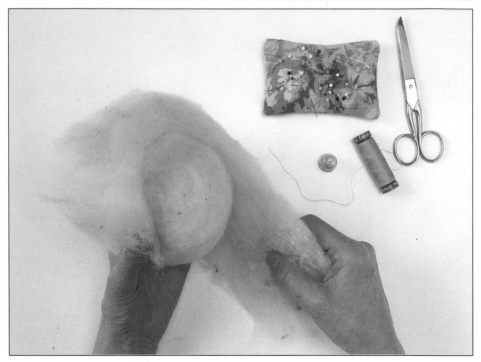

8 Roll some layers of wool batting one by one tightly around the ball of yarn, until it becomes the size of a fist. Secure the wool with a big pin and set it aside for the time being.

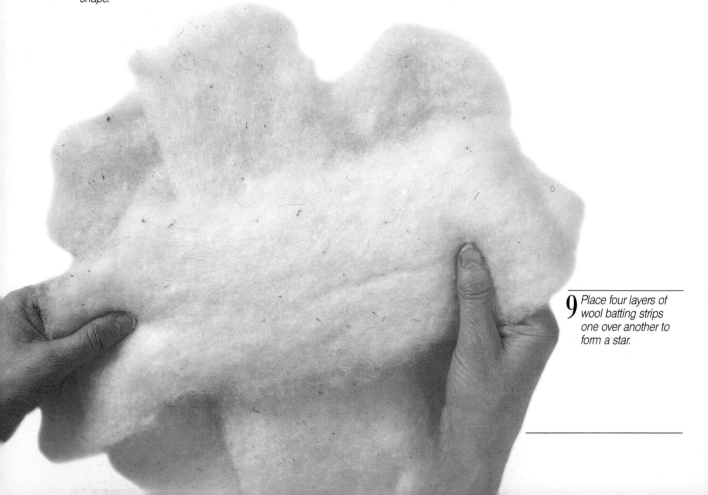

9 Place four layers of wool batting strips one over another to form a star.

10 *Place the ball you made in step 8 in the middle of the star of wool and envelop it completely.*

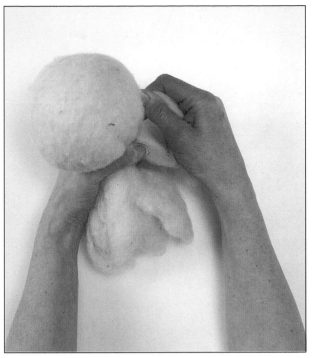

11 *Gather the edges of the layers of wool together and hold them tightly at what should already appear as the neck.*

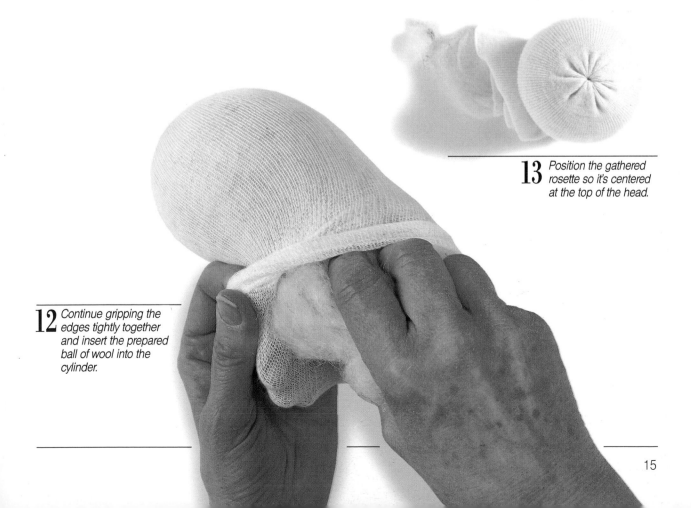

13 *Position the gathered rosette so it's centered at the top of the head.*

12 *Continue gripping the edges tightly together and insert the prepared ball of wool into the cylinder.*

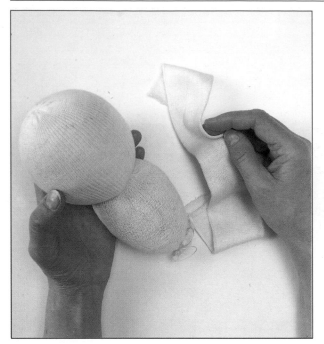

14 Tie the neck as high as possible with a piece of strong twine. As this binding-off will shape the neck and chin, it must be solid and even. Secure the lower end of the sock with a few stitches.

15 Push the bottom of the sock with force towards the head and secure it with some strong twine.

16 You now have a sort of swelling at the base of the head which will give shape to the shoulders. If the fabric has a seam, make sure it's placed at mid-shoulders.

17 Place the head on your work surface, with the seam facing you. Tie a piece of strong twine halfway across the height. This binding marks the eye sockets.

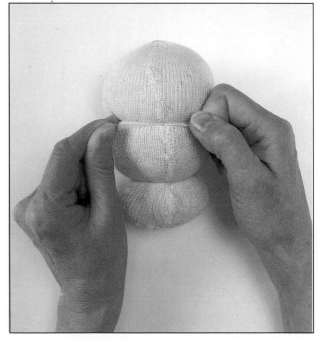

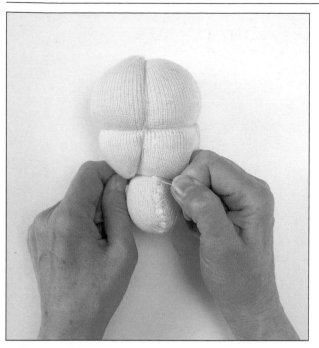

18 With the same piece of twine, tie the head halfway widthwise. The twine must go from the top of the head down along the point of the ears and end up with a knot under the chin. Tie it tightly, pushing the padding with your finger so as to create a well-defined chin.

19 You will now have two pieces of twine intersecting at the point for the ears. Make sure that the position corresponds to the eyes-ears line. Secure the crossing pieces of twine at these points with a few stitches, around them and through the fabric as well.

20 Now hold the doll's face in the palm of your left hand. With your right hand, lift the horizontal twine and pull it downwards until it reaches the neck binding.

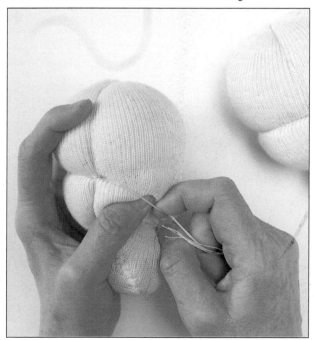

21 Hold the twine in this position with a few long stitches, and then set this part of the work aside.

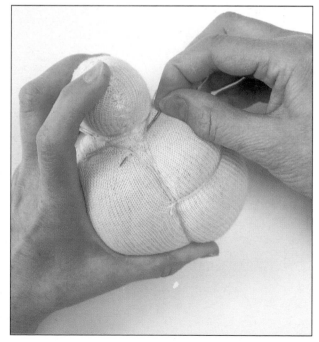

THE BODY

To make the body, you will need very fine knit fabric, whether purchased or remnants of old clothes. Depending on the size of your doll, 1/3 to 1/2 yard will be sufficient. Remember that the fabric is needed for the doll's skin, so if you're using remnants, be sure to pick a skin-tone color, not white.

22 Photocopy the patterns below, enlarging them to the size desired.

You may need to enlarge them in several steps, for example, 200%, then 150%.

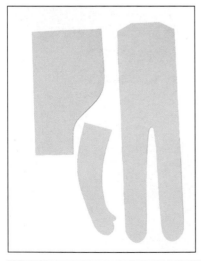

23 Fold the fabric in half lengthwise. Place the patterns on it, with the pattern for the head placed along the fold of the fabric. Mark the outline with a soft pencil or a piece of chalk and then remove the patterns.

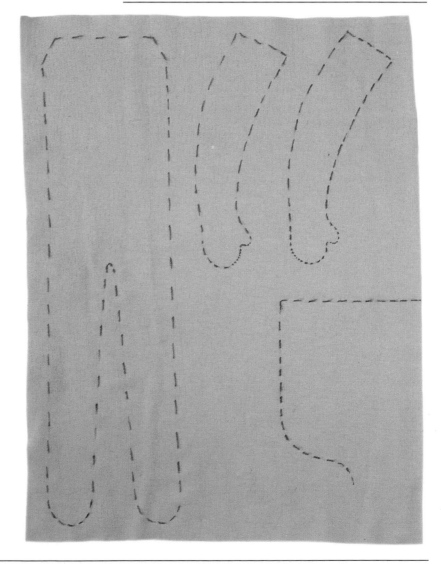

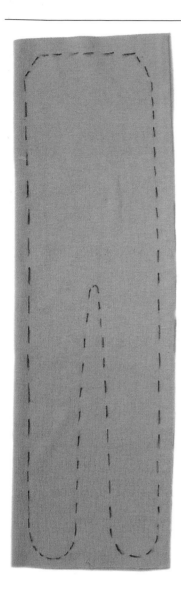

24 Baste the parts of the body following the outlines and then sew with a narrow zigzag stitch, leaving the top of the body, arms, and head open. Also leave the neck open. If you're sewing by hand, use a backstitch so your stitches will be secure yet flexible. Cut out the shapes leaving a 1/4" seam allowance all around.

25 Before turning the pieces right side out, make tiny snips along the curved parts to facilitate movement.

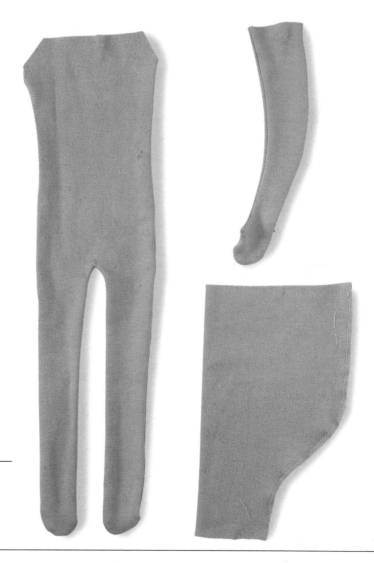

26 The pieces will seem tight and out of proportion. Don't worry: the knit fabric will stretch a lot in width as it is stuffed.

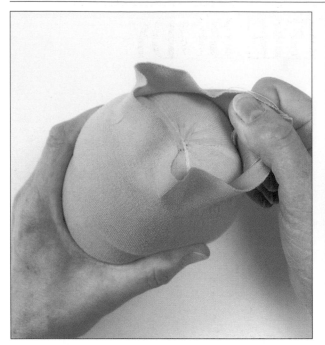

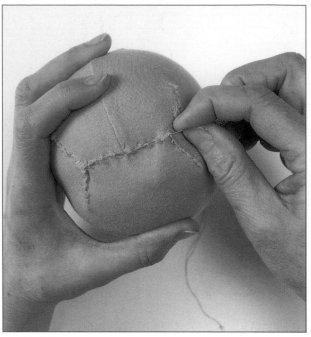

27 Insert the head set aside earlier into the prepared head piece. Make sure the smooth part of the fabric covers the face and that the seam falls in the middle of the back of the head.

28 Pull the top edges to cover the top of the head. Fold the fabric and secure it with small hand stitches. Cut away any overlapping parts that create too much thickness.

29 Stretch the fabric so that it adheres to the slight hollow of the eye socket. Pull it well under the chin, pushing it towards the nape of the neck, and tie it tightly with strong twine. Tie the bottom end, too.

PADDING THE BODY

30 *Now start padding the parts for the body. To make your work easier, turn a part of the fabric inside out and start filling it with wool batting, making sure to stuff the smaller parts such as fingers, hands and feet.*

31 *To prevent lumps from forming in the arms, roll some wool around your finger then push it firmly into the arm. Pull your finger out, leaving a cavity in the wool. Repeat this process until the arms are completely stuffed. Leave about 1 1/4" almost free of wool.*

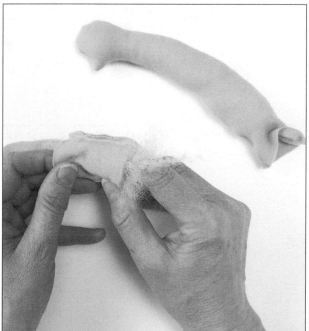

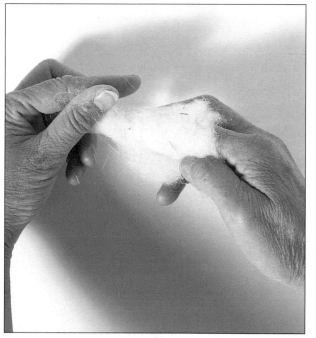

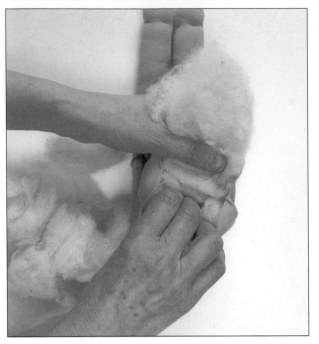

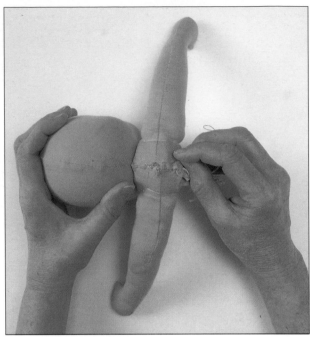

32 *Stuff the legs and then the body as far as the armpits. The legs will seem very long, but will be just right once you've formed the feet.*

33 *Now secure the two arms at the lower protuberance of the head by overlapping the two unpadded ends (for about 1 1/4"). Sew securely with thread doubled, passing the needle from one part to the other.*

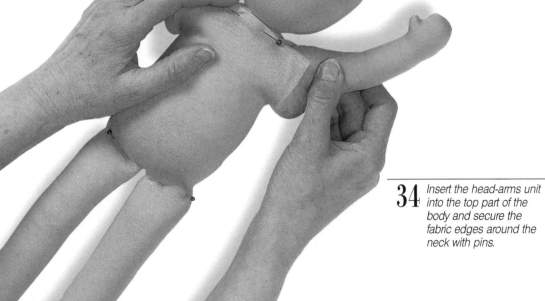

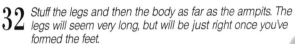

34 *Insert the head-arms unit into the top part of the body and secure the fabric edges around the neck with pins.*

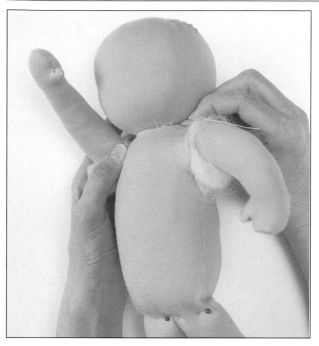

35 *Push any excess wool that emerges from the shoulder joint back into place.*

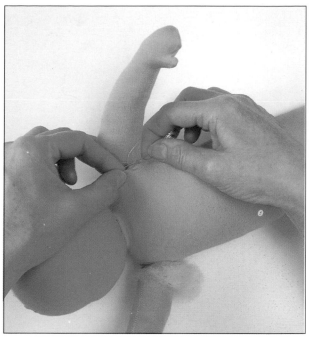

36 *Now sew the arms, shoulders and neck with small, close stitches.*

37 *There are two ways of sewing on the arms. If you sew them on when lowered, they are nicer to look at, but static.*

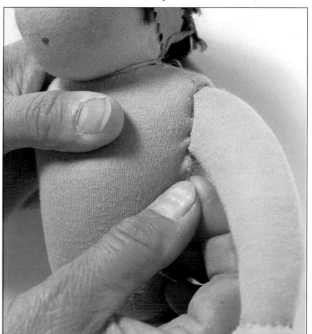

38 *If you opt for this idea, then make sure there is slightly more padding at the joints.*

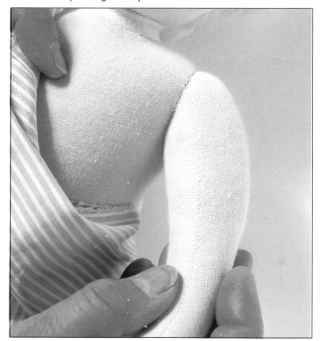

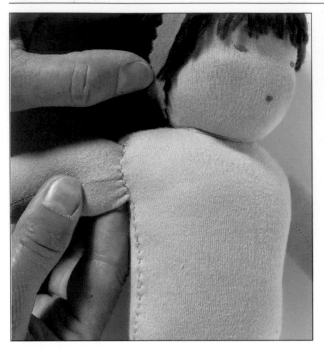

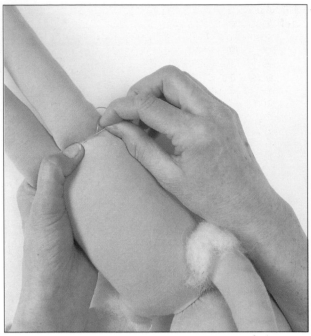

39 Or you could have arms which move. In this case stuff them less, and sew a flat seam while keeping the arms outstretched. The joining will be less attractive, but once dressed, the doll will be more natural-looking because her arms move.

40 The same goes for the legs. While inserting the wool with your fingers, create a hollow between the legs and the body. Sew a seam of small running stitches so that the legs will bend.

41 If instead you pad the legs in a uniform manner, they will be rigid.

42 Stitched seams at the knees allow movement, too. If hidden under rompers, they'll make the doll even sweeter-looking because you will be able to feel its soft legs bending as if they were real.

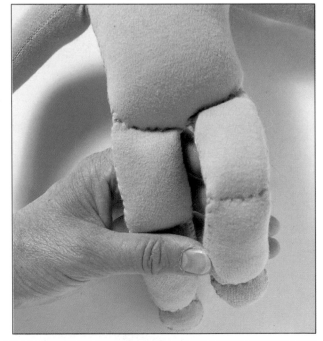

43 *A useful tip for the neck: if you want to hide the seam and elongate the neck a little, do not sink it completely into the body. When joining the head to the body, leave about 1/4" between the two parts. Fold a small strip of fabric in half and tie it around the neck. Pull it very taut before sewing it into place with a few stitches at the back.*

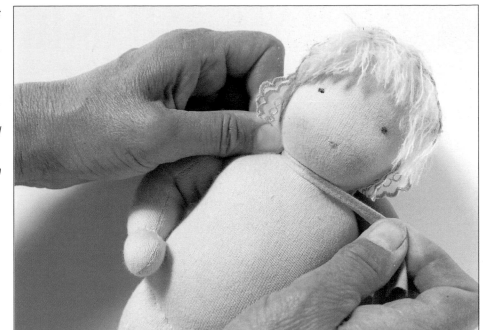

To shape the feet, bend the tip of the legs at a right angle. Secure them in this position by taking alternately one stitch from the fabric of the feet and one from the leg. Pull the thread tightly and then lock-stitch it.

44

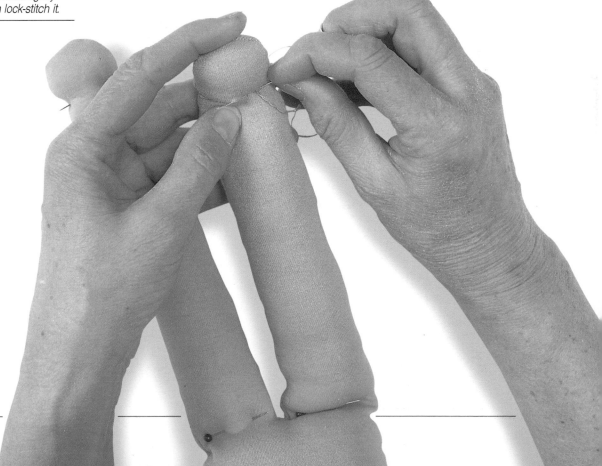

EYES AND HAIR

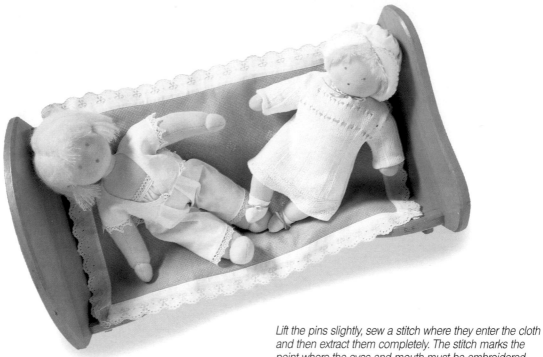

Before making the eyes, use pins with colored heads to try out their positioning. Use pale blue pins for the eyes and a red one for the mouth. This will help you to give the doll a more life-like expression. The eyes and mouth positions should form an equilateral triangle.

45

Lift the pins slightly, sew a stitch where they enter the cloth and then extract them completely. The stitch marks the point where the eyes and mouth must be embroidered. With a piece of embroidery thread and a sufficiently long needle, enter through the ear point and come out exactly where the eye is. Either sew several overlapping stitches so that the mark is clearly visible, or else sew small cross stitches to form a star. To make the mouth, sew one single stitch with a piece of pink thread.

46

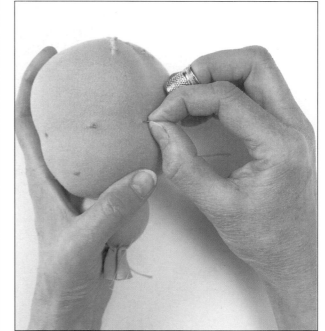

47 If you prefer, you can always use a colored pencil to make the eyes. Slightly wet the tip of a pale blue pencil and dot the spot where you had inserted the pins. Repeat this process several times until the eyes reach the size desired.

48 The mouth is nothing but a small, round pink dot.

49 Slightly color the cheeks with a piece of chalk or wax pastels, softening it towards the cheekbone

50 Now mark the hair line with a piece of thread and a running stitch.

51 Starting from this line, use long, closely-placed stitches to cover the top of the head with the wool chosen for your doll's hair. These stitches will prevent the scalp from being seen once the actual hair is applied.

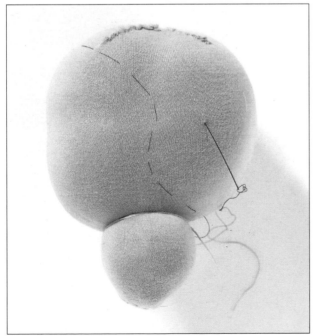

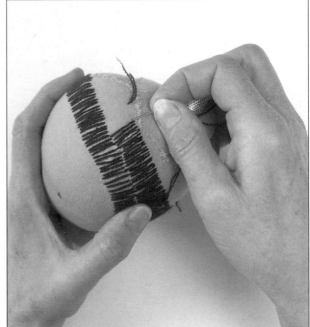

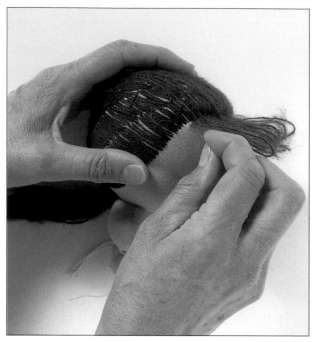

52 *Now insert the needle with a long thread. Beginning at the nape of the neck, sew a small stitch without securing it. Pull the thread, leaving a long tail, and sew another small stitch on the top of the head. Then enter and exit the needle on the forehead, along the first round of hair worked, without fastening the stitch, so as to form a loop.*

53 *Without extracting the needle, repeat the same operation backwards. Proceed in this way until you have created a series of rings on the forehead and the nape is completely covered by hair.*

54 *Arrange next to each other about 50 strands of wool of equal length. Lift them up together, as a unit, and center them on the head, so that an equal length falls each side. Secure them with small stitches at the top of the head, forming a seam which looks like a center hair part.*

55 *Sew a similar seam on the side, but secure only half the hair, leaving the rest to hang free.*

56 *At this point your doll's head will be covered with relatively long hair, and you can now give her the hairstyle of your choice. You can braid her hair, or roll it up around the ears. You can even cut it in a bob!*

Silk or viscose yarn can be used instead of wool, but while the hair is indeed glossier, these materials are more difficult to work with.

WASHING AND PRESERVING YOUR DOLL

Your handmade rag doll can be easily washed. While you are washing your child, soap the doll from head to toe. Rinse it well several times, then squeeze it gently to get rid of any excess water; leave it to dry. Do not machine-wash the doll. First, it would get damaged, but most importantly because a smaller child may get extremely upset. Don't forget that their doll is "their baby."

If the doll doesn't wear either time or water very well, don't worry, it is easy to set it right again. If the hair has started to thin out a bit or is a little damaged, then all you need to do is sew some more yarn onto the head. Use a piece of chalk to touch up the pink of the cheeks. Sew it another dress, and it will be as good as new.

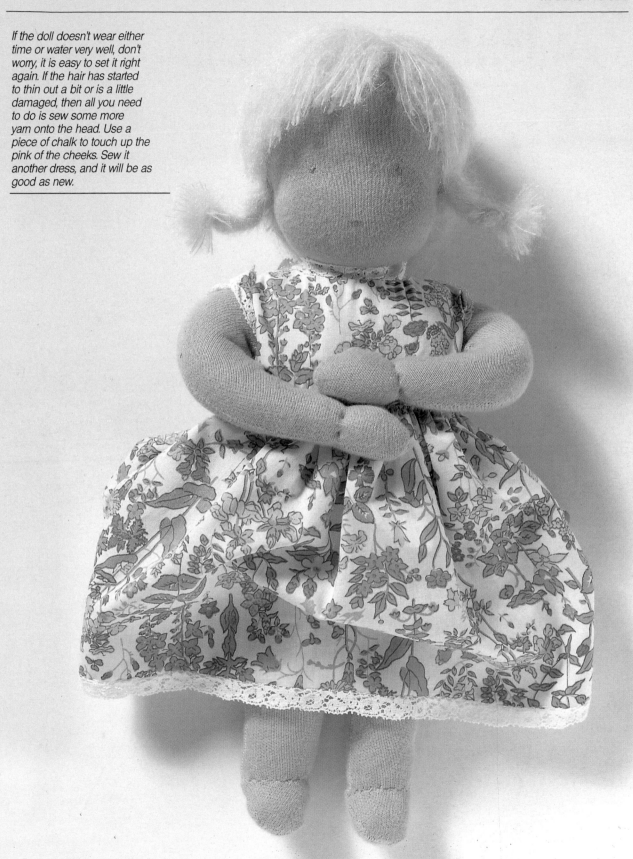

MAKING YOUR DOLL LOOK LIKE A BABY

Here are a few simple tips for making your doll look like a baby. It is often enough just to concentrate on the dress and the hairstyle for a doll to take on a different look. A baby generally has short hair, is a little on the chubby side, wears rompers or goes around barefooted. And babies often wear bonnets. Once you have made your doll, try fitting it out with different clothes. You can also slightly modify the shape of the legs by fixing the knees in a bent position, typical of newly-born babies. Here's how.

Bend the leg of the doll as far as the knee and secure it at the back with a few stitches, as you did to shape the feet (see page 25). The bent knees already gives the doll a cuter look. You can repeat this same technique for the arms.

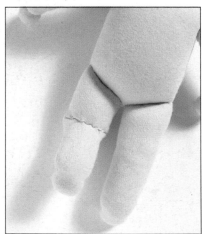

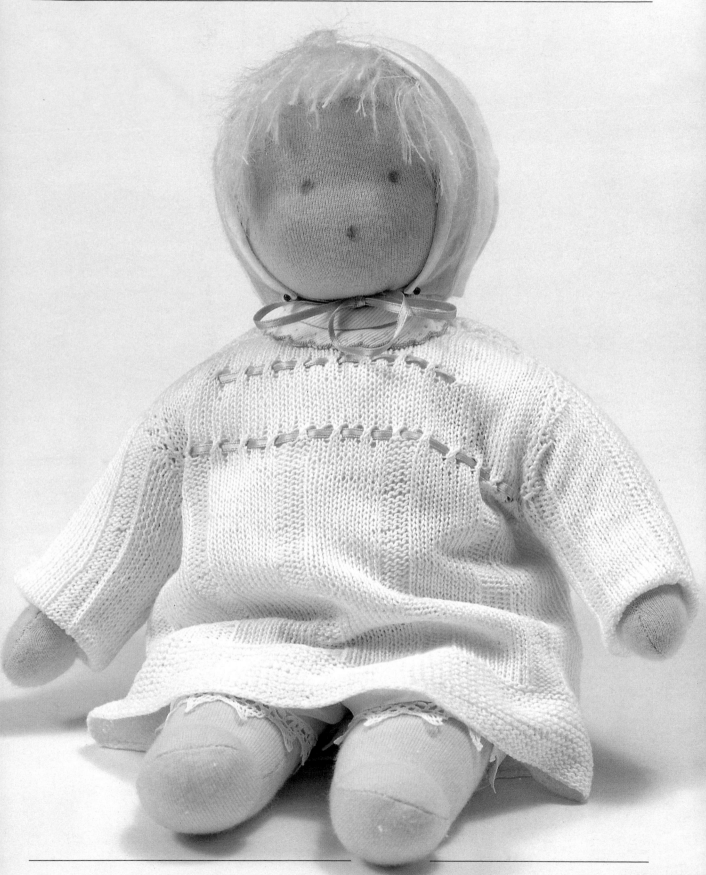

JUST LIKE A REAL NEWBORN INFANT

On the previous page we had a look at how to make a basic doll look like a baby. But you can also form a doll directly in the shape of a newborn infant. The doll-making techniques don't differ. What does vary is the shape of the legs and arms, the head is slightly bigger, and you must stuff the belly so it's rounded, which is so typical of babies.

1 *To make arms and legs that can move to and fro, it is necessary to work on each part separately. Cut 4 arms and 4 legs, developing the patterns from enlarged photocopies as you did for the basic doll pattern on page 18. Sew the various parts, pad them and stitch them individually. Cut the fabric for the body in one single piece with the head, making sure the seam remains at the back.*

2 *Insert the head as prepared on page 14 and stitch the top of the head closed. Stuff the body and stitch the bottom part closed. To define the neck, use the tip in step 43 on page 25.*

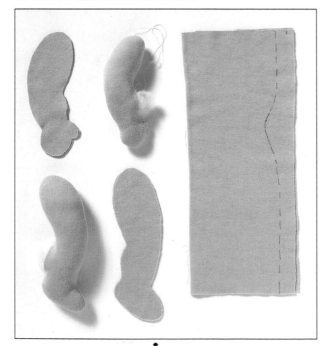

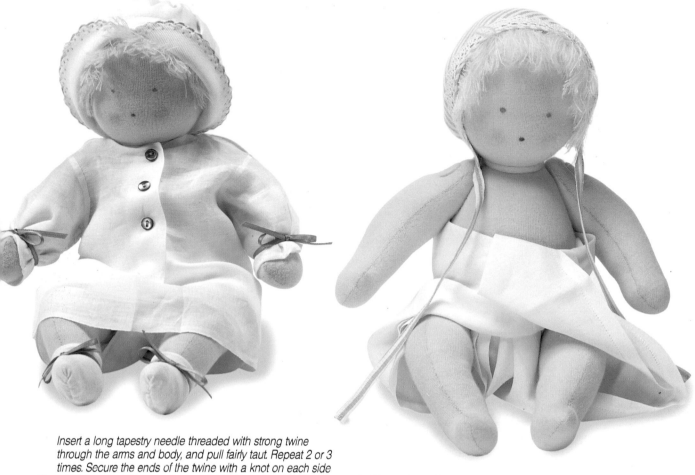

3 Insert a long tapestry needle threaded with strong twine through the arms and body, and pull fairly taut. Repeat 2 or 3 times. Secure the ends of the twine with a knot on each side which can be hidden under two flat fabric-covered buttons. Join the legs in the same way.

4 The arms and legs can now move and your baby doll can sit just like a real baby.

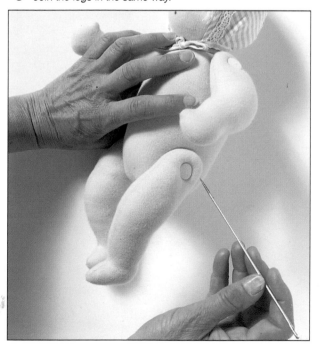

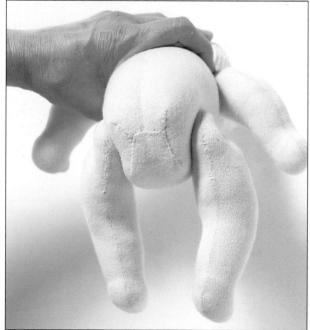

A BASIC PATTERN FOR DOLL CLOTHES

You have made some dolls and your children will surely want clothes to go with them. In the following pages you will find all the necessary step-by-step instructions for making clothes. To make garments that fit well, however, it is important that you measure your doll accurately and make a basic pattern, which can be your point of reference when making other doll clothes.

TAKING MEASUREMENTS AND DEVELOPING THE BASIC PATTERN

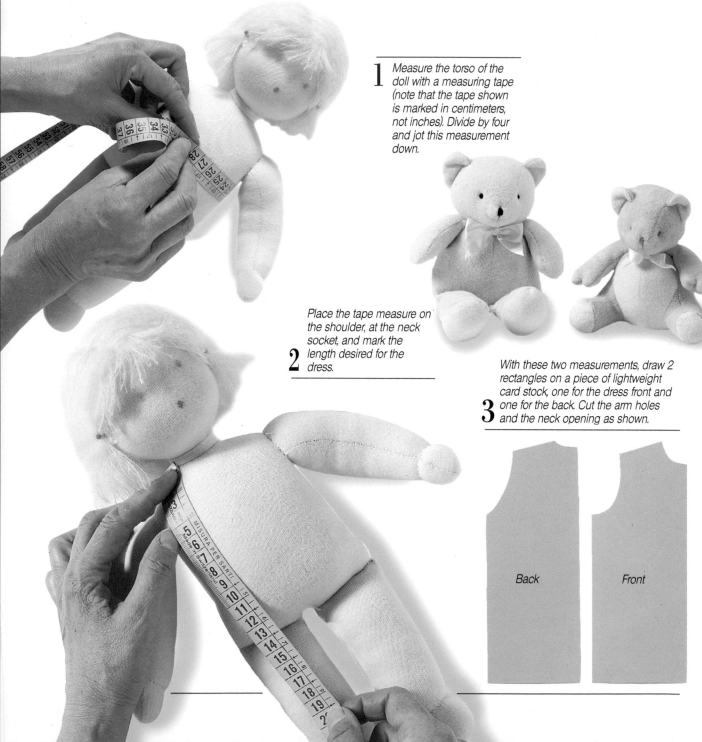

1 Measure the torso of the doll with a measuring tape (note that the tape shown is marked in centimeters, not inches). Divide by four and jot this measurement down.

2 Place the tape measure on the shoulder, at the neck socket, and mark the length desired for the dress.

3 With these two measurements, draw 2 rectangles on a piece of lightweight card stock, one for the dress front and one for the back. Cut the arm holes and the neck opening as shown.

Back   Front

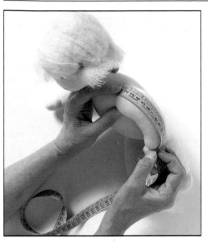

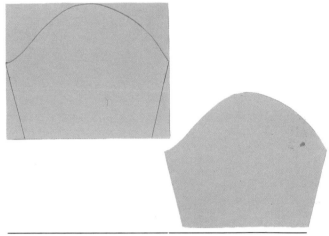

4 *Measure the length of the arm.*

6 *On a piece of lightweight card stock, draw a rectangle with these measurements. Referring to the photograph, trace or copy the curve of the arm joint. This is the basic pattern for the sleeve. When cutting out the fabric pieces, remember to leave 1/4" for seam allowances.*

5 *Now measure the circumference of the arm.*

PETTICOATS AND OLD FASHIONED KNICKERS

From a piece of cotton fabric, cut out a rectangle that is twice the waist measurement by the length from the waist to below the knees. Stitch the back center seam. On the top edge, insert elastic lace which will create gathering. Both the shoulder straps and the hem of the skirt are trimmed with lace. To make the flounce, make a 1/2" pleat about 1" from the bottom and stitch.

To make delightful little knickers, cut out a small arch of cloth at the center of the same pattern made for the skirt and stitch the crotch seam. Hem the legs, trim with lace, or insert elastic 1/2" from the bottom of the legs to make them even more attractive.

This small shoulder-strapped petticoat is the easiest you can make, and doesn't need patterns.

SLEEVELESS DRESSES

Take your basic pattern (described on page 38), and mark the length of the bodice.
Using the dress depicted on this page as an example, mark the outline of the neckline, noting the neck is lower on the bodice front than in the back.
Cut the shape of the bodice in tracing paper.
Widen the skirt to about double that of the basic dress pattern.

Now that you have your own patterns, cut the fabric, bearing in mind that it must be double. Remember to add 1/4" seam allowances as you cut. Prepare the fabric for the skirt as for the petticoat on page 40. Right sides together, sew the front and back bodice together at one underarm seam. Gather the skirt by sewing 2 rows of running stitches. Join the skirt to the bodice. Sew the other underarm seam and the side of the skirt. Finish by trimming the dress with lace.

Work buttonholes in the bodice front and sew small buttons to the back to close the dress at the shoulders.

DRESS WITH SQUARE YOKE

The white dress shown on page 43 can be dressed up with a lace yoke.

Fold a 4" long piece of 2"-wide lace in half and stitch diagonally to miter it. Trim the corner. Repeat and sew the 2 mitered pieces together to form a square. Cut an opening in the center for the neck, and trim with lace. Cut the back of the yoke open and trim with 3 buttons down the back to make it easier to dress the doll.

LONG-SLEEVED FELT DRESS

The bodice and sleeves of this felt dress are cut in one piece. The skirt is gathered the same way as the dress with yoke on page 44, but not so much because felt is more rigid and cumbersome than cotton.

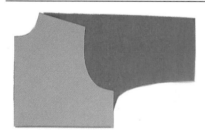

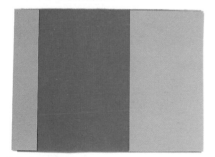

Place your basic pattern on tracing paper. Draw the waist line. Extend the sleeve by drawing a more rounded underarm. Cut out this new pattern. Use pinking shears to cut out the felt pieces, adding 1/4" seam allowances. Hand stitch the pieces with seams on the outside. Decorate with a felt heart and trims.

TYROLEAN JACKET

This Tyrolean jacket can be made using the same pattern as the felt bodice. Cut it a little wider and longer, and leave 1/2" extra on the front for overlapping. (Directions for blouse and jumper are on page 78.)

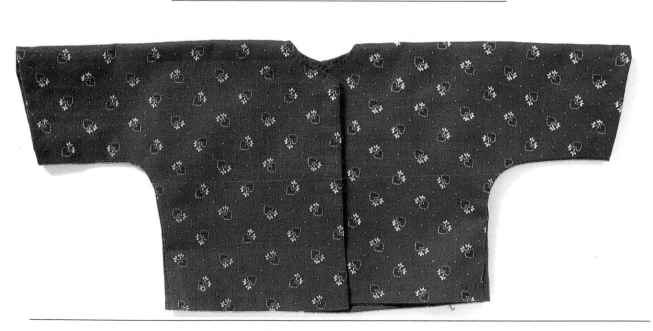

FELT ROMPERS

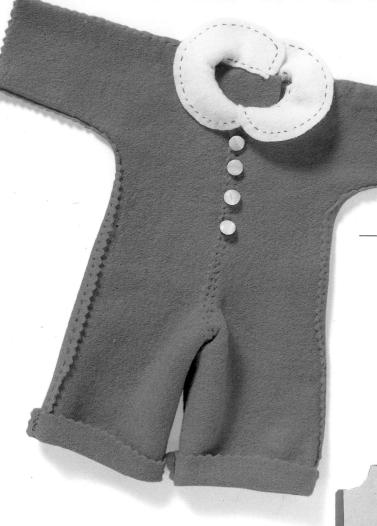

These rompers also can be made using your basic pattern.

Place the pattern on a piece of tracing paper and extend the drawing as far the doll's ankles. Lengthen the sleeves as you did for the felt dress on page 46 and add the crotch, as shown. Place the tracing paper on doubled fabric and cut out 2 pieces. Repeat, so you have 4 sections. First sew the inside of the legs, then the back seam and the crotch, leaving the front open. Use snaps or Velcro to close the front, and add buttons on top for decorations. Lastly sew the underarm/leg seam and the shoulder seams. This type of fabric does not fray as other materials do, so trimmings are not really necessary. If you want to give a finishing touch to your rompers, then you can cut the edges with pinking shears.

DUNGAREES AND BLOUSE

Add the point for the crotch to your basic pattern, as shown. Make the neckline and the armpits deep, as shown. Cut 4 overall sections.

Cut the white blouse as you cut the bodice of the felt dress on page 46. Cut felt pockets and flowers out of scraps.

Sew the inner leg seams, then the crotch. Finally, stitch the outer leg seams. Attach the pocket and decorate with felt flowers. Stitch buttons to the shoulder straps to secure them.

NIGHTDRESS WITH LACE INSERTS

Take your basic pattern and cut out one similar, but slightly flared at the bottom, as shown. Cut the front and back on folded fabric, but before sewing, apply the lace vertically with zigzag stitches. Trim away the fabric beneath the lace. Stitch the side and shoulder seams, then trim the neck and hem with lace.

This lawn dress is extremely elegant, and just slightly flared at the bottom.

The same pattern was used, only slightly longer, for the doll's christening dress. To allow for pleats as shown, cut the dress 1" to 2" wider than the pattern.

SHORT-SLEEVED FELT DRESS

Still using your main basic pattern, slightly widen the bottom part of the skirt, curve the arm hole a little and add long sleeves. Cut the front on the fold. For the buttons down the back, cut the back in 2 pieces, leaving 1/2" extra on each piece for overlap.

This is a dress you can make and decorate with felt hearts in 30 minutes.

EASY-TO-MAKE DRESSES

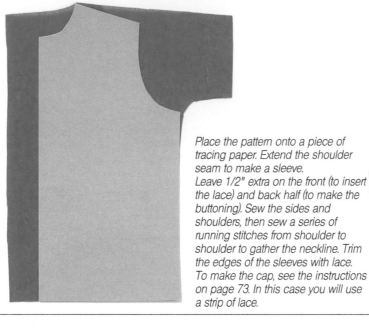

Place the pattern onto a piece of tracing paper. Extend the shoulder seam to make a sleeve.
Leave 1/2" extra on the front (to insert the lace) and back half (to make the buttoning). Sew the sides and shoulders, then sew a series of running stitches from shoulder to shoulder to gather the neckline. Trim the edges of the sleeves with lace.
To make the cap, see the instructions on page 73. In this case you will use a strip of lace.

Delightful little garments in floral and checked cotton.

LONG NIGHTDRESS WITH RUFFLE

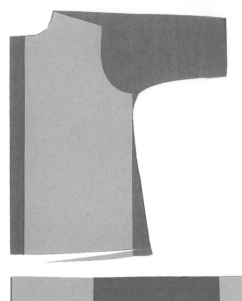

Place your basic pattern on tissue paper.
Flare the hem slightly and extend the shoulders
as you did the felt dress on page 46.
Extend the center front of the pattern 1/2"; cut the
front in 2 pieces.
The buttons on the front are hidden behind the lace.
Cut the back in one piece. To make the ruffle, cut a
strip 1 1/2" wide by twice the width of the hem. Trim
one long edge with lace. Sew 2 rows of running
stitches to gather the hem.

A SMALL
WARDROBE

FLORAL DRESS

A floral dress is suitable for a doll depicting a 1- or 2-year old girl. It is buttoned at the back.

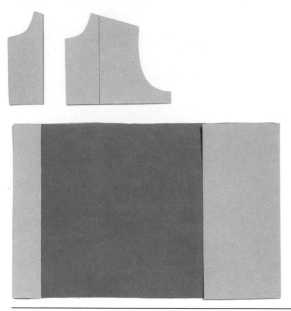

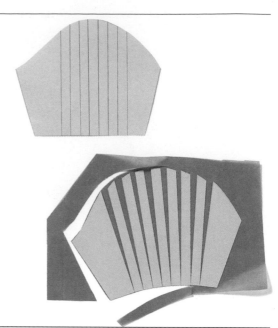

1 On your basic pattern mark the waistline and the shape of the white bib. Widen the skirt section so it is twice as wide as the waist measurement.

2 Using the pattern for the sleeve, draw about 8 vertical lines and cut along these lines, as shown. Arrange the parts on the tracing paper near to each other, spacing them about 3/8" to 1/4" apart at the top only: the space between the strips is needed to give the width necessary for gathering. Now cut the pattern of the new sleeve from tracing paper.

3 Place the front and back of the basic pattern so the shoulder edges are aligned as shown. Following the curve of the neckline, draw the shape of the collar and trace it on the tracing paper.

4 Now cut a fabric rectangle for the skirt.

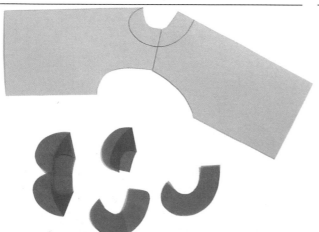

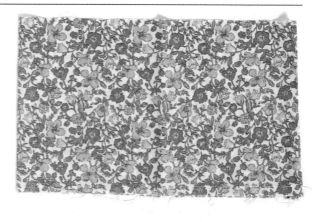

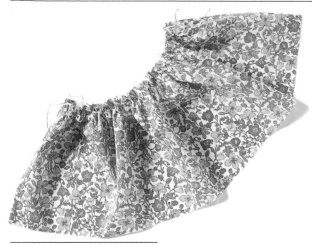

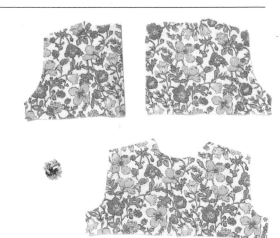

5 *Sew 2 rows of running stitches along one of the edges to gather it.*

6 *With the bodice pattern, cut the front on the fold (1 piece) and the back open in 2 pieces, leaving 1/2" to 3/4" to overlap for the buttons.*

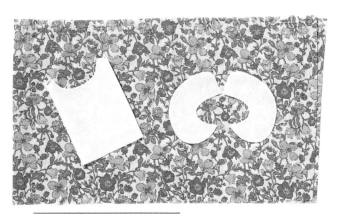

7 *Use the tracing paper patterns to cut the bib and the collar from white piqué.*

8 *Cut out the sleeves, placing the pattern on doubled fabric. Sew 2 rows of running stitches on the curved edge. Sew the underarm seam, then gather the sleeve top.*

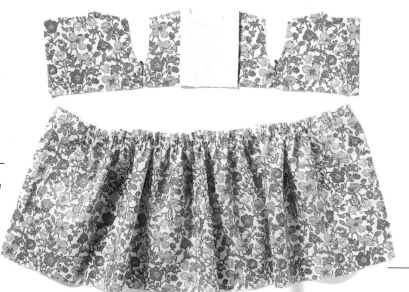

9 *Sew the underarm seams of the bodice. Then sew the white bib on the front of the bodice and attach the gathered skirt. Sew the shoulder seams, then set in the sleeves, keeping the part with the lower sleeve hole in the front.*

DRESS WITH SHORT BODICE

Here's another floral dress suitable for a "1-year-old" doll.

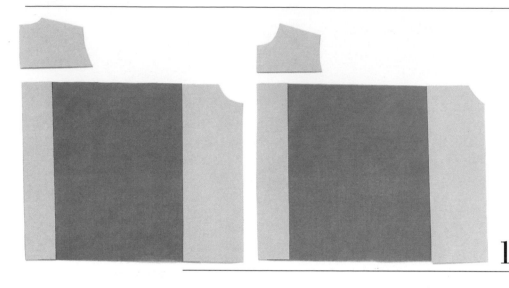

1 *Mark the length of the bodice on your basic pattern. Widen the skirt 2 1/2 times or as desired. Make the sleeves following the instructions on page 68 for the floral dress.*

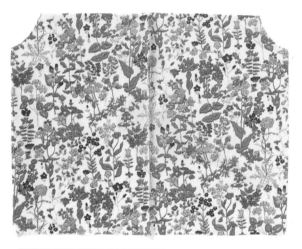

2 *Cut out the skirt front along the fold.*

3 *Cut the back in 2 pieces, leaving it open for sewing on the buttons.*

4 *Cut out the bodice front on the fold and 2 bodice back pieces.*

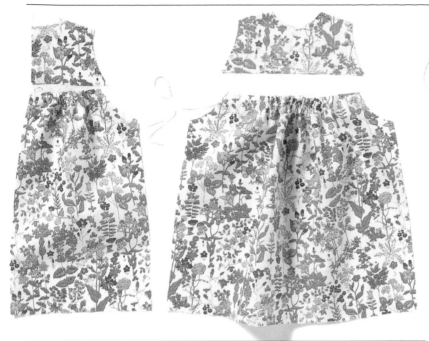

6 *Sew the sleeve seams and gather the sleeves by pulling the running stitches. Sew the sleeves to the bodice.*

5 *Sew 2 rows of running stitches along the top edges of the skirt pieces, and then gather and sew the pieces to the bodice, as shown. Sew the side and shoulder seams.*

Using an enlarged photocopy of the bonnet pieces shown below, trace the outline of the bonnet or draw it freehand. The straight side of the fabric strip is the front. Its length equals the length of the baby's face from cheek to cheek.

7

The rounded piece of the back must be sewed to the rounded part of the strip. Trim the cap with lace. Cut a strip of fabric to the needed length and stitch it to the bottom of the bonnet, leaving the ends free for tying.

8

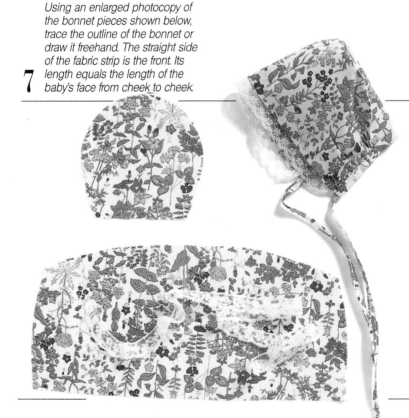

DRESS WITH LACE AND FOLDS

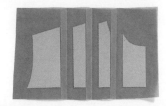

Prepare your pattern by making vertical snips on the bodice as shown above left. Leave about 5/8" between the strips for creating folds under which the lace is inserted.

The sleeves are very wide their whole length, not only at the shoulder joint like the dress on page 68. To gather them at the cuffs, sew elastic in them or simply tie them with lace as shown, opposite.

This is a different version of the previous dress, and it is for a "3- or 4-year-old" doll.

TYROLEAN DRESS COMPLETE WITH BLOUSE

The bootees are made following the instructions on page 102.

This Tyrolean dress presents a waist-length bodice. Pair it with a series of embroidered aprons and a white blouse.

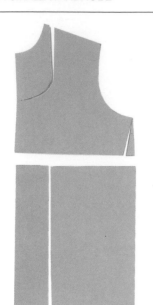

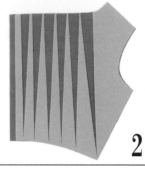

Develop your basic pattern further by cutting the waist length bodice. Shape the waist gradually, starting from the underarm. Mark the deep neckline and enlarge the sleeve hole slightly.

1

To make the blouse, cut a basic bodice and mark 5 or 6 diverging lines that start at the neck and widen towards the bottom, as shown.

2

Cut along the lines, place the pattern on tracing paper and widen the strips according to how much gathering you desire. Make the sleeves as indicated for the dress on page 66.

3

Enlarge the apron pattern and cut 1 from felt. Decorate it with small scraps. Button it in the back by crossing the shoulder straps.

4

DRESS WITH RUFFLE

This delightful little dress can be made following the instructions outlined for the previous dresses. The buttons are down the back. All you need to do is widen your basic pattern slightly towards the bottom, as you did for the nightdress on page 62. Add the ruffle and cut the sleeve as for the dress on page 68.

DRESS WITH PLEATS

1 On your basic pattern mark three parallel lines about 1/2" apart, running from the base of the skirt to the neck and shoulder. Cut and place the strips on the tracing paper, arranging them so that there is a 3/4" space for a fold between each.

2 With the new pattern cut the cloth but not the neck opening. Make the folds, baste them in place, then place the basic pattern on the dress and cut the neckline. The sleeves are made like those of the dress on page 64, but a little shorter. Trim them and the hemline with lace.

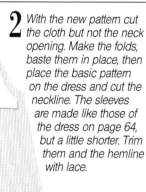

Lots of little pleats and puff sleeves make an adorable dress trimmed with bow-shaped buttons.

RIBBED AND FLORAL DRESS

This vivacious little dress is the result of recycling a pair of old socks. From a knee sock cut out a piece long enough for the bodice. Make two sleeves by cutting two rectangles of the right size from the other sock and sew them to the bodice (see page 38 for the basic pattern with the arm holes and the neck opening). The breadth of the skirt has to be twice the doll's chest measurement. While sewing the bodice to the skirt, stretch the sock fully. It will gather the skirt nicely. Trim the edges with lace. Leave the neck opening very wide so that the dress may be put on overhead.

THE LITTLE PRINCE

This cape, which is round, may be cut using a dinner plate as a template. At the center make a round hole big enough to fit the doll's neck, and then cut from the hole to the outer edge to make the front opening.

Cut one each of 2 contrasting fabrics. Stitch them right sides together, leaving the neck open. Turn right side out and bind the neck edge to finish. Add a button and loop closure.

The trousers are made like the dungarees on page 52, but without the bib.

The shirt is made like the dress on page 48.

You will probably have already read *The Little Prince* to your older children. So try to make this doll so that it looks like him!

A FELT COAT

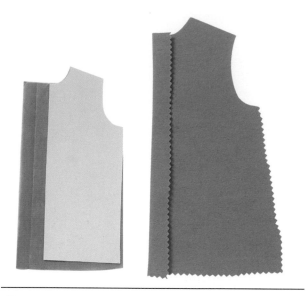

1 Make your basic pattern adding the space for buttons on the front and extra length, as shown.

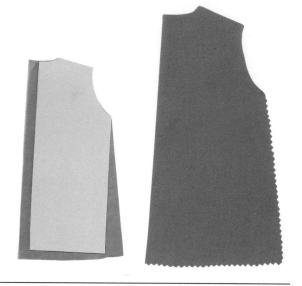

2 For the back, instead, leave half as much space to make a fold which will give width to the shoulders.

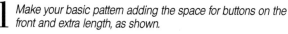

3 Cut an almost straight collar so that it fits well around the neck. Cut a second one, 1/4" larger from white felt and sew them together to the neckline.

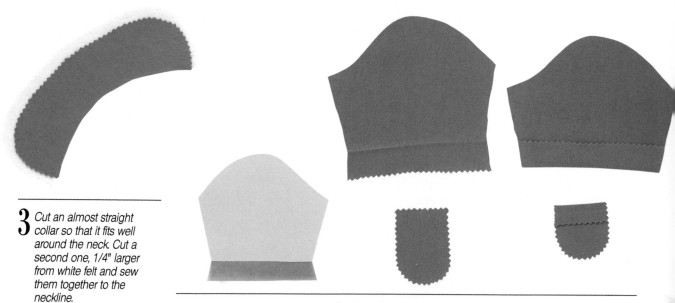

4 Make rather wide sleeves so that the coat can be easily slipped on over other clothes. Leave them long so that they can be turned back into cuffs. Cut out pockets in the same style as the sleeve cuffs. Use pinking shears so that all edges are finished off nicely. Cut buttonholes and add buttons to the front.

Here is a felt coat to wear on cool days. This coat is very easy to make. Simply cut the basic pattern a little wider so that the coat may be worn over the dress.

DRESS WITH BODICE AND SLEEVES IN ONE PIECE

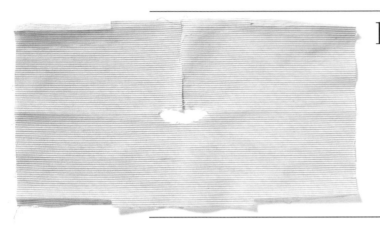

1 *Cut a rectangle measuring the length of the doll's outstretched arms from one hand to the other by the width of the sleeve. Make 2 snips 1/4" deep in line with each underarm. Cut the neckline at the center and the opening at the back for the buttons.*

2 *Add lace trim to the front, then sew the sleeve seams as far as the snips.*

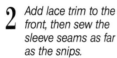

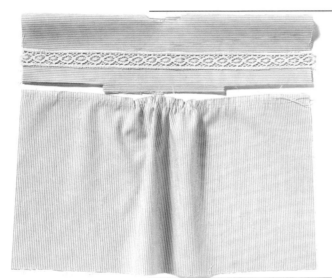

3 *Cut a skirt that is twice the doll's chest measurement; gather it and sew it to the front bodice.*

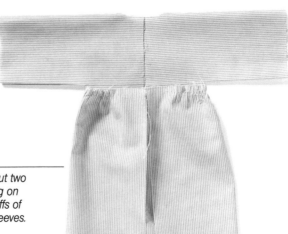

4 *Sew it to the back of the bodice too. Cut two strips about 1 1/4" and trim the opening on the back. To finish the dress, cut two cuffs of the same fabric and sew them to the sleeves. Sew lace to the hemline .*

These simple dresses, which can easily be washed and ironed, are open at the back.

The same pattern will look more sumptuous if made longer and from a piece of shimmering silk.

CHAMOIS LEATHER DRESS

The pattern of this dress is very simple as befits a young squaw. It is decorated with many beads and an equal amount of patience. To make the jacket, cut a rectangle measuring the length of the doll's outstretched arms from one hand to the other, by the width of the sleeve plus enough extra width to make a fringe. Snip the leather to make the fringe, and sew the sleeves, stopping 2" from the middle of the front. Decorate by sewing on one bead at a time with strong thread.

1

2 To make the dress, start from your basic pattern, widening it towards the bottom. Snip the hem to make fringe as you did for the jacket. Once on the doll, tie it at the waist with a belt. The dress could also be made with long sleeves that stick out from under the jacket with small fringed cuffs, as shown opposite. The leather chamois sold for cleaning cars is excellent for making this dress.

This dress is suitable for a doll with long, brown plaits and green eyes.

WARNING
Keep this doll out of reach of very small children because the beads can be dangerous if swallowed.

DRESS WITH A ROUND YOKE

This dress and romper with a round yoke is the most complex to cut, but the easiest to sew. Do not be discouraged by the patterns. It won't take you more than half an hour to sew it and it'll be worthwhile.

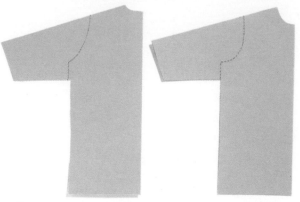
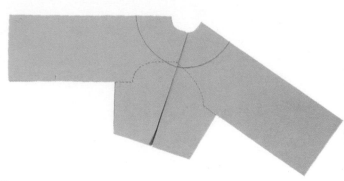

1 *Take your basic pattern and, placing a ruler on the shoulder line, extend it to make a long sleeve.*

2 *Place the front shoulder next to the back shoulder and draw the round yoke.*

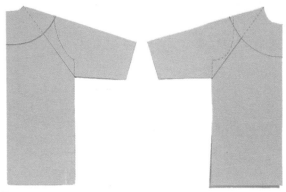
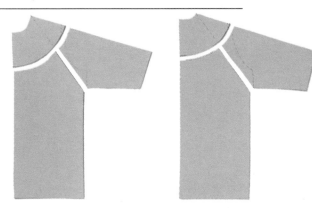

3 *Mark a line from the underarm towards the neckline, stopping at the yoke.*

Cut out the pieces.

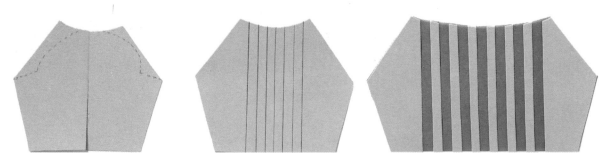

4 *Join the front and back sleeves to make a whole sleeve pattern. Mark vertical lines on it and cut the sleeve apart on the lines. Place the pieces on tracing paper with the space of a strip between each one of them.*

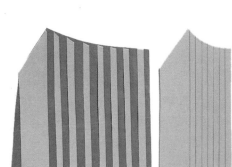
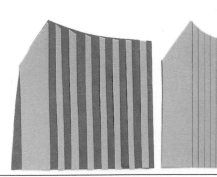

5 *Use the same process to widen the back and the front of the dress.*

6 With the new patterns, cut out the fabric. Sew the pieces together as shown and sew 2 rows of running stitches around the neck to gather the fabric.

Fit the yoke will around the neckline, adjusting the gathers to fit. Topstitch in place. Fold the dress with the front and back right sides together and **7** sew the side and sleeve seams.

Rompers can also be made with this pattern. All you need to do is lengthen the skirt and create the legs by removing an arch of cloth to make the crotch, as shown.

UNDERWEAR

Even if underwear remains unseen, children draw immense pleasure from dressing their dolls from head to toe. So why not make a little trousseau of underwear for your child's doll?

With the legs of your children's tights you can outfit the doll with tee-shirts, underpants and tights. Remove one foot from the tights. Cut it in the center approximately as far as half the length. Stitch the legs of the tights with zigzag stitches.

If the tights are embroidered down the sides you can make lovely tights for your doll with embroidery on each leg. Socks are elastic and are therefore suitable for different-sized dolls. The tee-shirt, made from the leg of a pair of tights, is given a wide neckline, thus making it easier to slip it over the doll's head. For newborn babies which have slightly bigger heads, you can make tee-shirts open at the back, just like their first item of clothing.

BOOTEES

A beautiful dress and coat are incomplete without dainty little booties. The foot of a doll obviously does not have the same form as that of a baby, but pretty doll booties are not difficult to make. Younger looking dolls will look more realistic if they're barefooted or sporting a pair of socks and a ribbon.

1 For half boots with flowers, enlarge the pattern below and cut out the pattern from felt.

2 Fold the felt in half and sew the top part (vamp) together, beginning near the pinked edge and ending at the toe.

3 Open it and sew it to the small oval that forms the sole. Fold down the cuff.

sole

vamp

vamp

cuff

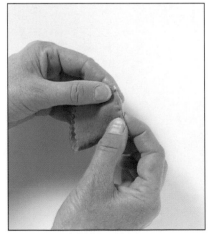

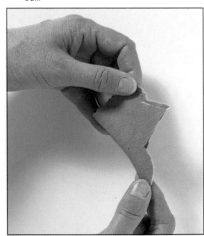

1 Choose one of the moccasin patterns above (the one on the right has cuffs), enlarge the pattern, and make 2 copies.

2 Cut the felt, lift the two end borders and overlap the sides. Sew to form almost a small box.

3 Insert and sew the tongue of the shoe which consists of the small oval.

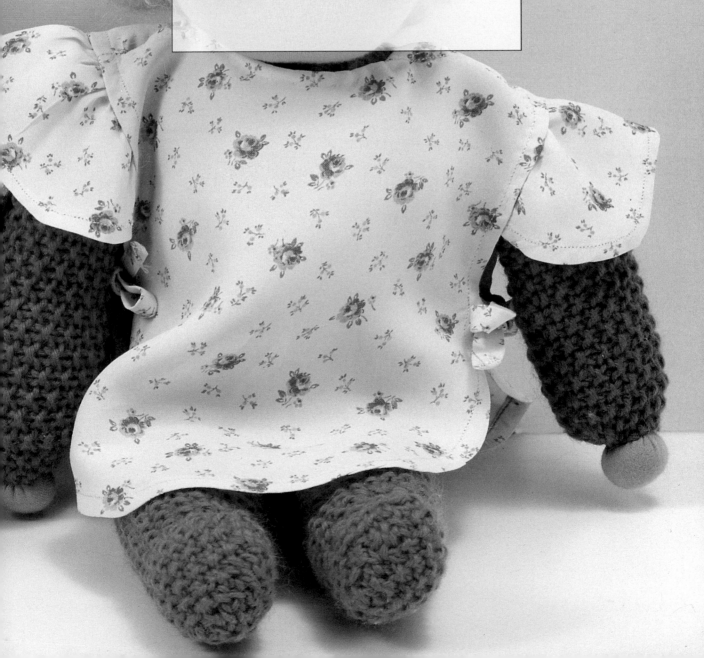

EASY-TO-MAKE DOLLS

DOLLS WITH PERMANENT CLOTHES

Time: 3 hours

A doll with a permanent outfit is suitable for very small children. Don't stuff it too full so it will stay very soft.

1 Enlarge the patterns above. Cut the fabric for the body, placing the enlarged pattern on folded fabric and leaving 1/4" extra for the seam allowances. To make the head, use pink fabric or better still, cotton doubleknit, even if a remnant.

2 Place one of the parts of the head on your work surface. Arrange on it parallel strands of woolen yarn which go vertically from one ear to the other, following the rounded top of the head down to the base of the neck (the central strands, the longest of all, will measure approximately 4"). Now place a second layer of about 1 1/2" long which will become the bangs. Cover the yarn with the second piece of the head. Holding the wool firmly, tack the two parts together and then sew with very small stitches, leaving a part of the neck open for turning.

4 Stuff the head with wool batting without pressing too hard. It must not feel hard but as soft as the rest of the body. Finish sewing the neck and tie a ribbon around it. Stuff the neck some more to make it rigid and stitch it closed.

3 Pull the wool through the neck opening, and turn the head right side out, stretching the hair well, which is now arranged along the line at the top of the head.

5 Comb the long hair to one side of the head to form the nape. To fix the hair, hold it in place with a couple of random stitches. Comb the short hair to the other side to create the bangs.

6 Paint or embroider the eyes and mouth and color the cheeks pink.

7 If you would like a doll with braids, work them separately and then sew them to the back of the head, hiding the seam under the other hair.

8 Now sew the body, leaving a space open in which to insert the head. Turn the work right side out and stuff it slightly. Insert the neck in the body and arrange the wool in the front and back of the doll so that the neck disappears. Attach the head to the body by hand with solid stitches.

WOOLEN DOLL

Time: 15 minutes

This is the oldest type of cloth doll. Fabric can be used instead of skeins of wool.

1 *You'll need one skein of wool.*

2 *Fold it at about three fifths of the length. Grip well with your hands at two fifths of the new length, as shown.*

3 *Wrap a strand of thick thread or wool tightly around this point to shape the neck. Give it a couple of turns, keeping the thread taut.*

Wrap a strand of the same thick wool at three different points around one of the sections, bringing it forward to make the arm. Tie the thread around the wrist and return to the starting point with the same movement backwards. Repeat this process to make the other arm. Make your way back to the back of the doll and give the strand a couple of turns around the neck. Pass it diagonally from the nape of the neck to the ear. Give it a couple of turns around the forehead to simulate a ribbon.

4 Divide the shorter part of the wool still left folded behind into two sections for arms.

5

6 Without cutting the strand, tie it first around the neck and then around the body, slightly under the armpits, to mark the waist.

KNITTED DOLL

Time: 6 hours

The head of this doll is similar to the one on page 12. If, however, you would rather make a quicker version, see page 108.

1 *For the knitted body cast on 42 stitches with No. 3 knitting needles and suitable wool, such as sport weight. Knit garter stitch (knitting every row) for 15 rows. Make a buttonhole at the center horizontally by casting off 8 stitches on the next row, then casting on 8 stitches on the following row. Knit another 15 rows, then cast off 14 stitches at both sides. Cast on 8 stitches on each side and continue knitting for another 30 rows. Divide the work in half and work each part for 36 rows. Cast off one stitch at each side of both legs and two stitches at the center until no stitches remain.*

2 *Fold and tack the pieces to form   the arms and legs. Using the same fabric as for the head, prepare two small stuffed balls for the hands and sew them on with small stitches, fastening them well to the sleeves. Sew the whole body together except the back.*

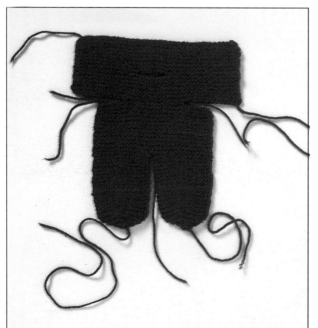

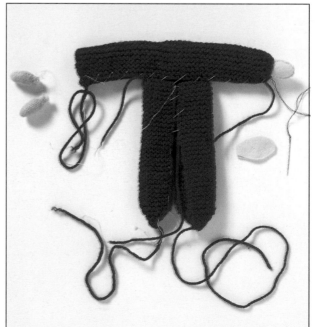

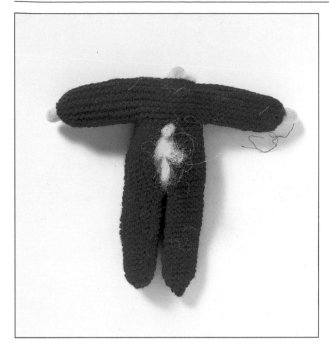

3 Stuff the whole body with wool, shaping it as you stuff it. Remember that knitted work gives a lot. Try not to stuff the wool too tightly and to spread it evenly. Fasten on the head, which must have a rather long neck for stability to the body, with small stitches.

4 Thanks to the give in knitted work, it is possible to obtain different shapes. The round tummy of this gnome and her chubby feet can be created by just stuffing more wool in the parts to puff a bit. The head is the same as that of the doll on page 12, with appropriate stuffing changes. Make the nose by inserting a small cloth ball before covering the head with the final piece of doubleknit.

The knitted doll may also be dressed, but a small pinafore is more than enough to add extra charm. Cut the pinafore in two separate pieces and hem the neckline and the outside edges. Attach the cap sleeves only at the shoulders. Ribbons and buttons fasten the neck and the waist.

DOLL IN A BAG

Time: 3 hours

These dolls are suitable for very small children. Here two gaily colored bibs are used instead of dresses.

The pattern for these dolls is a simple rectangle, gathered at the bottom to soften and round the shape. When making these pink and blue twins, mount their hands upwards. A row of running stitches for gathering the bag gives it the look of a dress. However, you could also make small colored overalls like those of the knitted dolls on page 112.

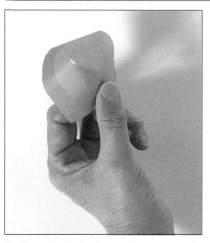

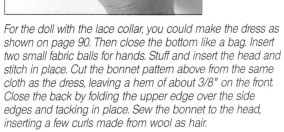

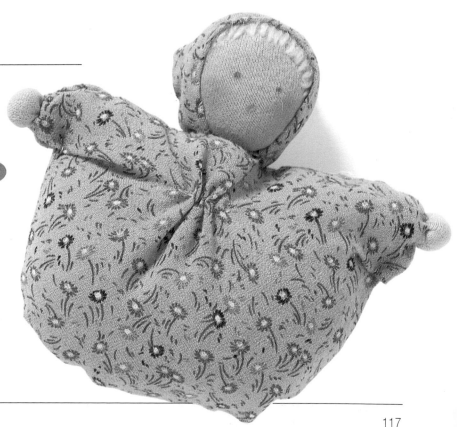

For the doll with the lace collar, you could make the dress as shown on page 90. Then close the bottom like a bag. Insert two small fabric balls for hands. Stuff and insert the head and stitch in place. Cut the bonnet pattern above from the same cloth as the dress, leaving a hem of about 3/8" on the front. Close the back by folding the upper edge over the side edges and tacking in place. Sew the bonnet to the head, inserting a few curls made from wool as hair.

For the doll in pink, cut 2 pieces using the pattern below and stitch them together, leaving an opening at the neck. Turn right side out and insert the head; stitch it in place. Make two small stuffed fabric balls for the hands. Insert these turned outwards.

DOLL IN A RICE-STUFFED BAG

Time: 1 hour

For the head, stuff a small cylinder of doubleknit fabric with a small ball of wool. Draw on the eyes and mouth. The body is made up of a rectangle of cotton with two knots at the upper edges which look like two little hands.
Half fill with rice and coarse sand, then insert the head and stitch in place.

To define the outline of the body, tie a band of trimming around the waist.

A simple bonnet of the same cloth as that used for the body finishes off the doll harmoniously.

The doll will assume different positions according to how the stuffing moves.

ON ALL FOURS

Time: 3 hours

Your bigger children will enjoy these two tiny dolls on all fours.

1 *Make a small head like the one on page 12 or, to simplify matters, you could make a small ball of wool covered in doubleknit. Cut out the body from an old sock and stuff it slightly.*

2 *Cut out a dress. Cut and sew the legs as described for the knickers on page 40. Slip the garment over the body, fastening it well at the neck, wrists and ankles.*

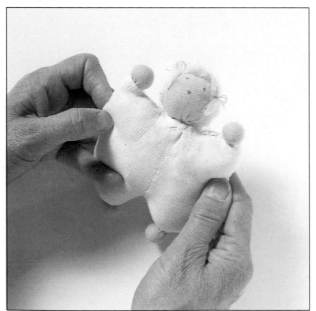

The doll looks extremely adorable even from behind with its plump little bottom as if it were wearing diapers.

3 *To achieve the "on all fours" effect, draw the two arms together and fasten them with some hidden stitches.*

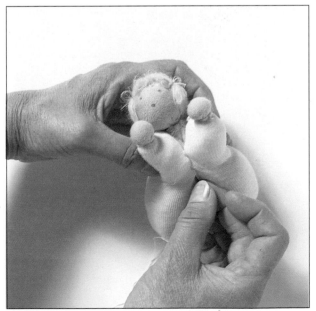

CRADLE, PUPPETS
AND OTHER TOYS

WICKER CRADLE

1 Purchase a basket big enough to hold your doll.

2 Cut a strip of fabric as long as the upper circumference of the basket and as wide as its height. Edge it with lace and sew it around a piece of cloth which has been cut to the same size as the bottom of the basket.

3 Insert into the basket three pieces of willow or other flexible material through the holes in the lace as shown in the photo and attach them with some strong twine.

4 Tie a string on the piece that will serve as the hood of the cradle and pass it around the others, fixing it to each with a knot. Tie the string to the foot of the cradle.

Cover the rods with a piece of fabric to form the hood. Stuff a small mattress the same shape as the bottom of the basket and add a pillow. Then make three bows of the same material to adorn the foot and sides of the cradle.

Any basket or chest can be turned into a cradle with a little mattress and a pillow.

WOODEN CRADLE

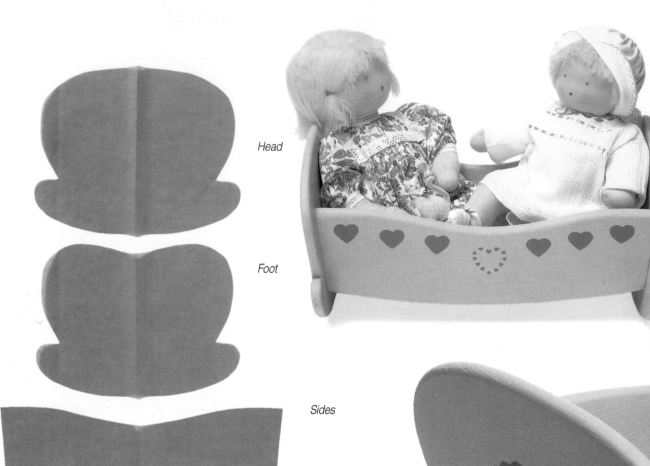

Head

Foot

Sides

Bottom

Enlarge the patterns to the size desired and cut
them accurately. Place them on wood or plywood,
and cut them out carefully with a jigsaw.
Using wood glue, glue the sides to the head, add
the bottom and then the foot. The cradle is quite
strong glued in this manner, but you could
strengthen it further with a few nails, passing from
the head to the sides.
Prime and paint the cradle, then use a heart-shaped
stencil to decorate the cradle.

As bed clothes for the cradle, make the little mattress, the pillow, a blanket, a sheet. An attractive bed cover will add the final attractive touch just like for real beds.

To make the mattress, measure the bottom of the cradle and cut two rectangles, adding 1/4" extra on each side for the seams. Leave one of the short sides open to insert the stuffing (wool or cotton). Then close with small stitches.

Work the little pillow in the same way in the appropriate proportions. This could be decorated with an edge of gathered lace.

The blanket can be made from a rectangle knitted with thick soft wool.

For the light cotton sheet, calculate the length and width generously so that it can be easily tucked in.

Last of all the bed cover. Cut out a rectangle of Aida cloth bigger than the size of the cradle. Decorate it with Sangallo lace (to round this at the corners, make various tiny folds).
On a sheet of squared paper trace out a little heart or cut one out from one of the many magazines on embroidery. Transpose the drawing to the Aida material according to your taste and embroider it in cross-stitch.

This romantic coverlet has pink hearts embroidered in cross stitch and cotton lace stitched around the edges.

PUPPETS

By making heads as on page 12, you can also create puppets for little shows. Classical characters such as kings, princes, princesses and pages are accompanied here by the frog to represent the famous fairy tale. The characters don't have actual clothes, nor a body. There is in fact only the cloak to which threads are tied to give the appearance of life to each puppet. A shirt with a bib is sewn nearly to the neck and will move when the arms are pulled by the threads manipulated by you.

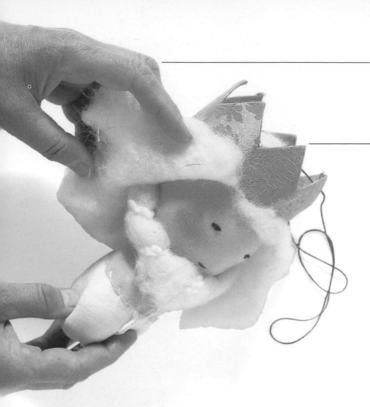

Make the head of your character with rather a long neck.
Instead of making the hair and beard as for the doll, you could just
sew on layers of wool batting.

Sew a rough outline of a shirt, and attach two small fabric balls for
the hands at the ends of the sleeves. Sew a row of running
stitches around the neckline to create some gathering.
Cut the king's clothes in velvet. This will simply be a big tunic
without sleeves and with a wide opening on each side from which
the shirt sleeves will emerge. Prepare a golden bib from some left
over trimmings. Then cut a wide silk rectangle to form a cloak.
Sew the shirt around the king's neck, then slip on the tunic and
pull out the sleeves through the openings. Fasten the bib to the
neck with a few stitches.
Gather the cloak a little at the nape of the neck and sew it to the
neck. Attach the cloak to the hands, and attach heavy threads to
the hands and the head. Cover a paper crown with gold-colored
fabric and your king is ready for the show.

The prince's cloak is made of electric-blue silk. The midnight blue bonnet is enhanced by a trimming cord.

The page is dressed in velvet of different colors. His bonnet boasts a small green feather stuck on with a drop of glue.

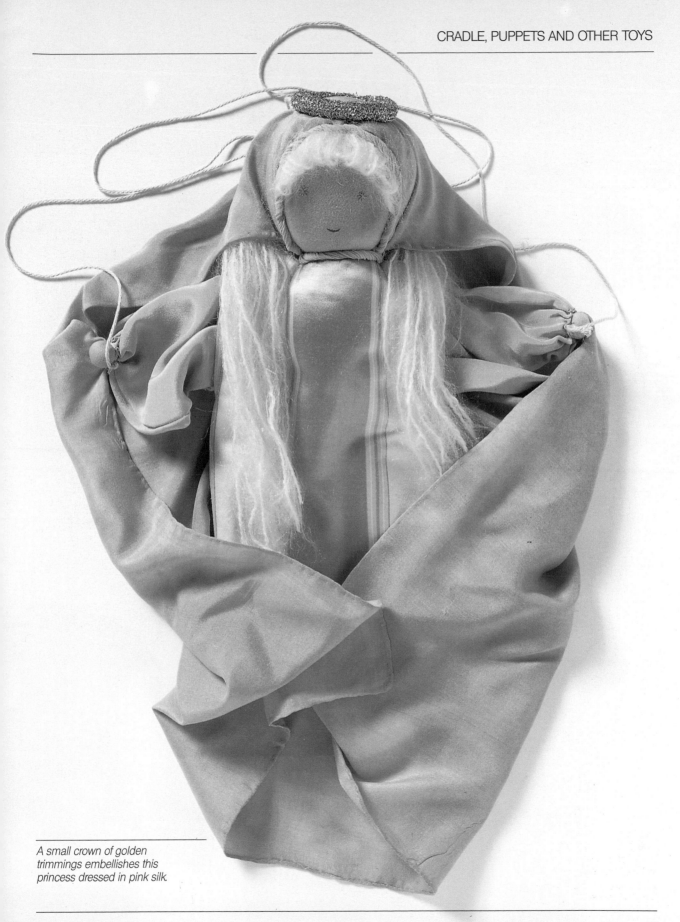

A small crown of golden
trimmings embellishes this
princess dressed in pink silk.

MAGIC CONE

The magic cone is an amusing toy for younger children. They will love to see the little sprite pop up and then disappear. You can create this movement by inserting a wooden dowel inside the cylinder.

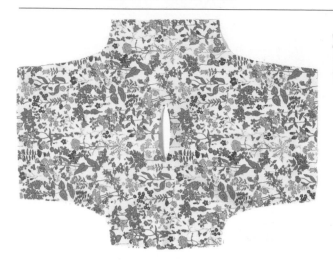

1 Enlarge the pattern at left so that the width at the bottom is 5", and cut it out of lightweight fabric. Cut a slit for the neck opening. Fold in half and sew the sides. Make two small hands of stuffed felt and fasten them to the gathered shirt wrists.

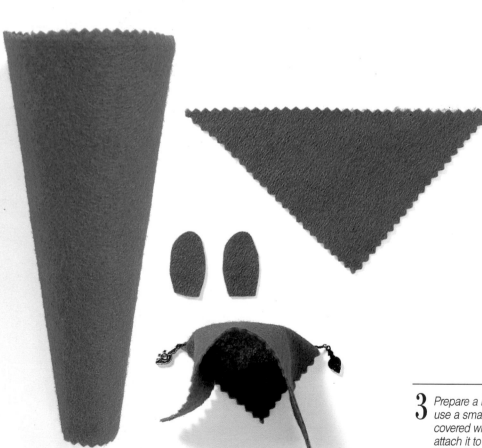

2 Prepare a cardboard cone with its larger circumference measuring 9 1/2" and the smaller one 2 3/4". Its height must be 7 1/2" inches. Spread it with glue and cover it with felt or cotton fabric.

3 Prepare a head (you could use a small wooden ball covered with knit fabric) and attach it to the top end of a wooden dowel, as shown. Make the head gear with a felt triangle and attach two little bells or two charms. Fasten it on the head with a few stitches or glue.

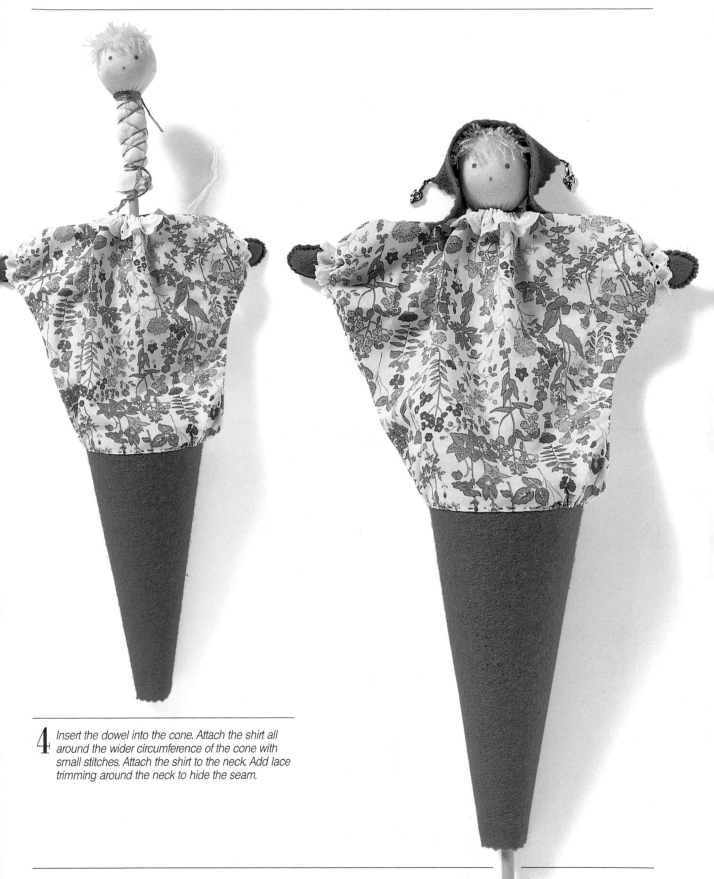

4 Insert the dowel into the cone. Attach the shirt all
around the wider circumference of the cone with
small stitches. Attach the shirt to the neck. Add lace
trimming around the neck to hide the seam.

CLOTH BOOK

This book proves fascinating for young children. It can be leafed through like a real book, but it is soft and flexible with no sharp corners. When planning your book, think of illustrating in it a fairy tale, a book of animals or all sorts of images with which you could make up different stories as you turn the pages with your child. Cut some rectangles of cotton about 23 1/2" long and 11 3/4" wide. Each rectangle represents a double page. From books or magazines, cut out outlines of animals, trees or cuddly toys. Use these as patterns for your decorations. By using different materials, you can obtain varied effects.

A duckling strolling across the meadow.

Dolphins leaping through the sea foam

The large goose in the pond among the cattails is made of felt as are the children with the ducks.

Different effects may be obtained by using gauze over velvet as shown here for the big moon in the night sky, which was sewn on by hand with tiny stitches. For the sailboat use cotton fabric, which you could machine appliqué using a zigzag stitch.

To make the figures on the left, cut out shapes leaving a 1/4"
margin. Tack them on to the material and stitch around the edge
with a narrow zigzag stitch. Trim the edge as near as possible to
the seam. Appliquéd cotton pieces require more time than the felt
ones, which do not ravel, but cotton has the advantage of being
machine washable.

Shapes in relief are also suitable for your book. The little doll is stitched on by hand. Stuff it by inserting a little cotton or wool under the material as you proceed in the stitching.

Once the decorations have been finished, join the rectangles of cotton two by two to form the pages of the book. Place two rectangles right sides together, with the decorations inside, and sew all around leaving a 4" opening for turning. Prepare all the pages in this manner, iron them, layer one on top of the other and stitch at the center for the book binding

TINKLING BELLS

With a few fabric scraps and a lot of love you can make most attractive colored balls. Before closing the last seam you could insert a little jingle bell which will add to its charm. If you use stretch terrycloth or jersey, the balls will be especially easy to make because of the give in the fabric. Enlarge the wedge pattern and cut out 8 pieces in different colors. Stitch them together, leaving an opening between the first and last piece. Stuff with polyfil or wool, pressing well, and then close the opening with a few hand stitches.

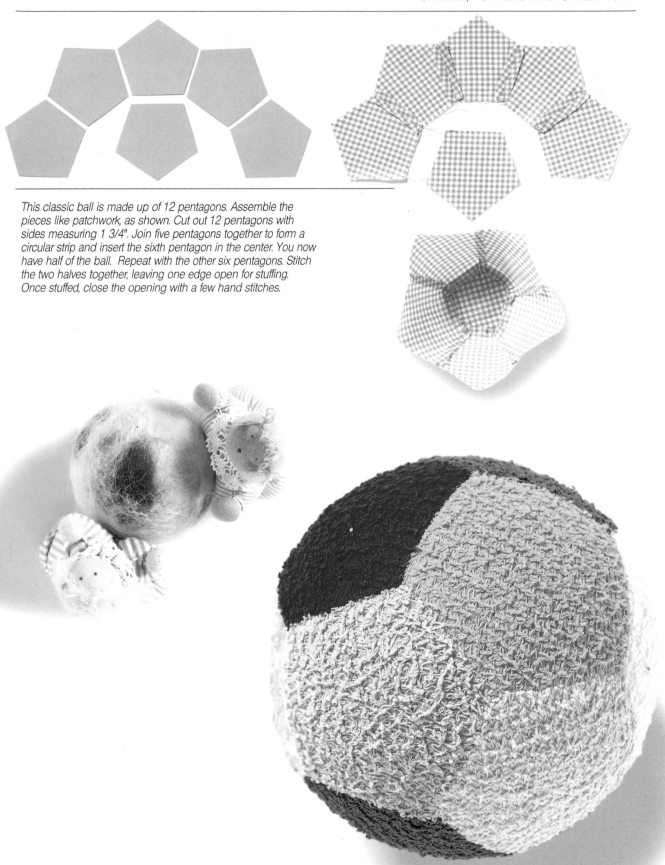

This classic ball is made up of 12 pentagons. Assemble the pieces like patchwork, as shown. Cut out 12 pentagons with sides measuring 1 3/4". Join five pentagons together to form a circular strip and insert the sixth pentagon in the center. You now have half of the ball. Repeat with the other six pentagons. Stitch the two halves together, leaving one edge open for stuffing. Once stuffed, close the opening with a few hand stitches.

LOTS OF GAILY COLORED ANIMALS

A DUCK

This chubby duck is made in floral material.
Enlarge the pattern at right as desired. Cut out 2 pieces from fabric, allowing 1/4" on all sides for seam allowances.
Sew the two sides together, leaving the bottom open; snip around the curved edges. Turn right side out and stuff through the bottom opening. Hand stitch the opening closed.

A GOOSE

This plaid goose looks handsome in his bow.
Enlarge the pattern at right and cut 2 of fabric, allowing 1/4" all
around for seam allowances. After stitching, make small snips
along the curved edges so that the work can easily be turned
right side out. Stuff and close as for the duck, opposite.

A TEDDY BEAR

Work the teddy bear the same way as the goose and dress him up with this charming little waistcoat cut from felt. Enlarge the patterns. Cut the cloth, sew and lightly stuff head and body separately (the bear is almost flat). Form the ears with a row of stitching. Insert the head into the body and attach it with small stitches. To make the front paws point upwards, sew a row of running stitches around the neck and pull the thread as you gradually fasten on the head.

LITTLE COLORED BEARS

Here we have almost completely flat bears in all sorts of colors. Enlarge the pattern as desired and cut 2 from fabric. Stitch, leaving one outer leg open for turning. Snip around the corners, then turn and stuff lightly.

PINK BUNNY

Enlarge the patterns as desired, and cut 2 rabbits and 4 ears from fabric. Sew the ears and turn them right side out, then fold the bottom and fasten the fold with a stitch. With the same technique used for the doll with the permanent clothes (see page 106) insert the ears as you did there for the hair. Stitch the bunny, leaving an opening. Turn it right side out and stuff it. Separate the legs with a row of stitching. Embroider the face details.

A COW

You can make this cow from patchwork fabric, as shown, or any print fabric. Prepare the patchwork, if desired. Enlarge the pattern and cut 2 cows from your fabric. Cut a few strands of jute or yarn for a tail, and place the tail between the two pieces of cloth. When the work is turned right side out, the tail will be already fixed in the right place. Saw the pieces together, leaving an opening for turning, clip the curves, turn and stuff.

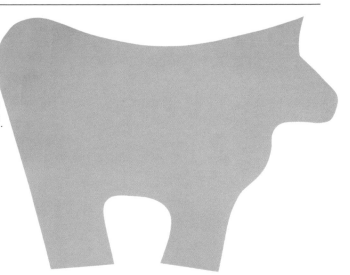

A SMALL FELT ZOO

This series of animals can be made by directly photocopying the shapes to make your patterns. They are in felt and stuffed very slightly.

Cut the following pieces separately and insert them between the two layers of cloth for the body before sewing:

• the dinosaur's mane
• the dog's ears
• the cat's tail
• the pig's tail
• the elephant's tail

Felt doesn't ravel so you can sew it directly on the right side. It's not necessary to turn inside out.

Therefore you can cut the shapes without leaving any seam allowances. However, stitch as close as possible to the edges. Add more animals to your zoo by getting other pictures from magazines and newspapers.